How to Deal with ADHD

Kids' Health™

Lynette Robbins

PowerKiDS press™

New York

For Lucy

Published in 2010 by The Rosen Publishing Group, Inc.
29 East 21st Street, New York, NY 10010

First Edition

Editor: Joanne Randolph
Book Design: Kate Laczynski
Photo Researcher: Jessica Gerweck

Photo Credits: Cover, p. 1 Mary Kate Denny/Getty Images; p. 4 Superstudio/Getty Images; p. 6 Ryan McVay/Getty Images; p. 8 Siri Stafford/Getty Images; p. 10 Yellow Dog Productions/Getty Images; p. 12 Holloway/Getty Images; p. 14 Shutterstock.com; p. 16 photos_alyson/Getty Images; p. 18 Kevin Cooley/Getty Images; p. 20 Adie Bush/Getty Images.

Library of Congress Cataloging-in-Publication Data

Robbins, Lynette.
  How to deal with ADHD / Lynette Robbins. — 1st ed.
     p. cm. — (Kids' health)
  Includes index.
  ISBN 978-1-4042-8140-0 (lib. bdg.) — ISBN 978-1-4358-3416-3 (pbk.) — ISBN 978-1-4358-3417-0 (6-pack)
  1. Attention-deficit hyperactivity disorder—Juvenile literature. I. Title.
  RJ506.H9R626 2010
  618.92'8589—dc22
                                        2009006412

Manufactured in the United States of America

CONTENTS

Me and ADHD

Andy has always had a lot of energy. When he was in preschool, he could not sit still and listen to stories like the other kids. In kindergarten, he was always getting in trouble for talking without raising his hand. In first grade, Andy had problems learning to read and doing his work.

Even though Andy was a bright boy, by second grade, he was far behind the other kids. He did not like school at all. Andy's second-grade teacher wondered if he had ADHD. "ADHD" stands for "attention-deficit/hyperactivity disorder." Kids with ADHD often have trouble sitting still and paying attention.

Like Andy, Nicolle has a hard time paying attention in class. She often finds herself drawing pictures or writing her name over and over rather than doing her class work.

Why Can't I Pay Attention?

Emily tried to **focus** on her math homework, but she could not keep her mind on the problems. She heard her mom in the kitchen and wondered what was for dinner. She saw a bird outside and made up a story in her mind about it. She got up to sharpen her pencil three times. Half an hour later, Emily had still not done a single problem.

People who have ADHD have trouble focusing on one thing for very long. They are easily **distracted**. Listening and following instructions is also hard for them. These problems can make it hard for a person with ADHD to learn new things.

Try to do your homework in a quiet place.
This will help you stay focused on the job at hand.

Why Can't I Sit Still?

Owen does not like sitting still. In class, he **fidgets** all the time. He is always leaving his seat without permission, too. At recess, Owen sometimes plays a little too hard and hurts other children.

People who have ADHD are often **hyperactive**. When "hyper" is at the beginning of a word, it means "very." People who are hyperactive are very active. They need to keep moving and have trouble sitting still. People with ADHD may also be **impulsive**. That means they often act before they think. Children who are impulsive may get **frustrated** and angry easily. They may also do things that could put them in danger, such as running across a busy street.

Playing a sport can be one way for kids with ADHD to use their energy in a positive way.

ADHD at Home

Caleb is late for school again. It took him half an hour to get dressed because he kept getting distracted by the toys in his room. Then he could not find one of his shoes. At breakfast, he spilled his juice all over his shirt and had to change. Caleb's mom is frustrated and his sister is annoyed with him.

It can be hard to live with someone who has ADHD. Family members may find it hard to be patient. The person who has ADHD may feel bad for not behaving better. It is important for everyone to remember that having ADHD is not your fault. It can be hard, but there are ways to make things better.

Talk with your mother or father about things that are hard for you. By working together, you can come up with a plan to make some things go more smoothly.

Greg's paper was a mess. Instead of doing his spelling, he had drawn pictures of airplanes and aliens. His desk was a mess, too. There were balled-up papers, broken pencils, and even food from old lunches in there. Greg knew that he would have to stay in at recess to finish his work.

Not being able to pay attention can make school very hard for children with ADHD. They may have trouble finishing assignments and listening to the teacher. They also have trouble keeping their things **organized**. They may forget things and lose assignments. A child with ADHD may get frustrated and stop trying.

To help you focus in class, ask the teacher if you can sit up front. Ask if you can get homework early in the week, too, so you have more time to work on it.

ADHD and Friends

Jake and Cody both have ADHD. Jake is always full of energy. He makes lots of jokes and does funny things. He is fun to be around. Jake has a lot of friends. Cody gets angry easily. He does not like to wait his turn. Sometimes, he hits other kids. Cody does not have many friends.

Like Jake, some kids with ADHD make friends easily. Other kids with ADHD are more like Cody. They have trouble making and keeping friends. They may have a hard time working with others and playing fairly. Kids like Cody may need help dealing with their feelings of frustration and anger. They need **strategies** that will help them learn how to behave around others.

Having ADHD should not keep you from making friends. Try to find activities that make use of your extra energy, then ask other children to join you.

Which Kind?

There are three main types of ADHD. Children who have the hyperactive type of ADHD are always moving. They have problems sitting still or doing quiet activities. They may also have a hard time controlling their impulses.

Children who have the **inattentive** type of ADHD may not actually be hyperactive, but they have trouble paying attention and finishing schoolwork. They may also have problems keeping things organized and remembering things.

The third type of ADHD is a mix of the first two types. Children with this type of ADHD are both hyperactive and easily distracted.

Jackson has the third kind of ADHD. He has a hard time sitting in his chair in school, and he gets distracted easily by what other students are doing.

What Can I Do?

If you have ADHD, there are many things you can do to make your life easier. Often, kids with ADHD meet with a **counselor**. A counselor can give you and your parents ideas and teach you skills that will help you **manage** your ADHD. Your teacher can also help. He or she may be able to make changes in the classroom that will make it easier for you to learn. Sitting in the front of the class can be one helpful strategy. This helps a child with ADHD focus on the teacher with fewer distractions.

What people with ADHD eat can also change the way they act. Some children are able to focus more if they do not eat foods with a lot of chemicals, or added matter, in them.

Have someone help you make a list of what you need to do each day. Taking things one step at a time can help people with ADHD follow through and finish their work. **19**

Taking My Medicine

A doctor will often **prescribe** a special kind of pill for a child with ADHD. These pills are a kind of drug called **stimulants**. They start to work in about half an hour. Most kids take their pills in the morning. The medicine helps a person with ADHD calm down and focus. This kind of medicine can make a big difference for many children.

Lucy had trouble listening and working at school. When she started taking medicine to help her ADHD, she was surprised at how much easier it was to do her work. Soon she was finishing almost all her work!

Having to take pills every day may seem hard and unfair. Try to remember that your pills will help you control your feelings and focus better.

Often, children with ADHD think that they are stupid. This is not true! Children with ADHD are just as smart as kids who do not have it. However, children with ADHD do have some extra challenges. If you have ADHD, your parents, teachers, and other adults can help you learn skills to manage your ADHD.

It is also good to remember that there are some good things about having ADHD. Children with ADHD are often very imaginative, funny, and **creative**! They may be good at sports or make good leaders. What special talents do you have?

GLOSSARY

counselor (KOWN-seh-ler) Someone who talks with people about their feelings and problems. A counselor also gives advice.

creative (kree-AY-tiv) Having different, new ideas.

distracted (dih-STRAKT-ed) Unable to pay attention to one thing.

fidgets (FIH-jets) Moves around a lot.

focus (FOH-kis) To pay attention to or concentrate on one thing.

frustrated (FRUS-trayt-ed) Upset.

hyperactive (hy-per-AK-tiv) Having a lot of energy.

impulsive (im-PUL-siv) Acting without thinking about what will happen.

inattentive (in-uh-TEN-tiv) Not paying attention.

manage (MAN-ij) To control.

organized (OR-guh-nyzd) Has things neat and in order.

prescribe (prih-SKRYB) To order medicine for someone. Only a doctor can do this.

stimulants (STIM-yuh-lunts) Medicines that make part of the brain more active.

strategies (STRA-tuh-jeez) Plans or different ways of handling something.

INDEX

WEB SITES

Due to the changing nature of Internet links, PowerKids Press has developed an online list of Web sites related to the subject of this book. This site is updated regularly. Please use this link to access the list: www.powerkidslinks.com/heal/adhd/